MOZART
SELECTED VARIATIONS

Edited and R  ew Edwards

To access companion recorded performances online, visit:
www.halleonard.com/mylibrary

"Enter Code"
1538-2902-3382-6428

On the cover:
The Dance
by Nicolas Lancret
(1690–1743)
© Hermitage, St. Petersburg, Russia/The Bridgeman Art Library

ISBN 978-1-4234-8387-8

G. SCHIRMER, *Inc.*

DISTRIBUTED BY

 HAL•LEONARD®

7777 W. BLUEMOUND RD. P.O. BOX 13819 MILWAUKEE, WI 53213

www.halleonard.com

Contact us:
Hal Leonard
7777 West Bluemound Road
Milwaukee, WI 53213
Email: info@halleonard.com

In Europe, contact:
Hal Leonard Europe Limited
42 Wigmore Street
Marylebone, London, W1U 2RN
Email: info@halleonardeurope.com

In Australia, contact:
Hal Leonard Australia Pty. Ltd.
4 Lentara Court
Cheltenham, Victoria, 3192 Australia
Email: info@halleonard.com.au

CONTENTS

The price of this publication includes access to companion recorded performances online, for download or streaming, using the unique code found on the title page. Visit **www.halleonard.com/mylibrary** and enter the access code.

HISTORICAL NOTES

WOLFGANG AMADEUS MOZART (1756–1791)

Few names in history are as recognizable as that of Wolfgang Amadeus Mozart, the *wunderkind* of the Classical era. Once a composer whose popularity rose and fell regularly, he now holds a place among the greatest names in music, and rightfully so. His music can be found literally everywhere—from symphony halls to third grade classrooms—all around the world. Scholars and musicians far and wide have pored over his works, his writings, and his life, describing in great detail the style of his writing, the influences upon it, and what elements exist that make it seemingly perfect. Yet his music not only attracts all manner of *intelligentsia*, it also finds an immediate place in the hearts and minds of trained and untrained musicians alike. It is this kind of universal appeal that ultimately lifts Mozart to the high pedestal upon which he resides.

His instinct was discovered quite early, as he began playing chords at age three, and improvised short keyboard pieces by age five. Soon the talents of Wolfgang and his sister Nannerl caught the attention of wealthy and influential families in Munich and Vienna. Their father Leopold, seeing the opportunity, arranged an extensive tour of Europe in 1763; the young composer would often write works in the carriage to pass the time as they traveled. By 1767, Wolfgang was receiving serious commissions, including a funeral cantata and a Latin opera. It is in this early part of his career that the first set of variations in this edition were written. Generally speaking, the writing from this early period is in the gallant style of the pre-Classical works of Carl Philipp Emanuel Bach and others.

In 1773 Mozart returned to Salzburg, and began a prolific compositional period. Already with well over 100 works to his credit, Mozart began to achieve a mature style, refining and expanding the natural gifts that had displayed themselves so early in his work. In one sense, the music that the average listener recognizes as "Mozart's sound" emerges in this period.

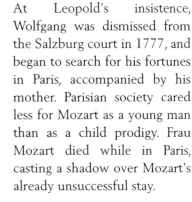

At Leopold's insistence, Wolfgang was dismissed from the Salzburg court in 1777, and began to search for his fortunes in Paris, accompanied by his mother. Parisian society cared less for Mozart as a young man than as a child prodigy. Frau Mozart died while in Paris, casting a shadow over Mozart's already unsuccessful stay.

The 1780s and a move to Vienna brought a degree of independence and success through commissioned works; Mozart also managed to find some regular income by taking on students in both piano and composition. In 1782 he married Constanze Weber, the sister of his former love Aloysia. During his periods of success, the family was able to acquire a taste for the luxuries of a fine household. Yet as his commissions rose and fell with the fashion of the day, the Mozart family income often bordered precipitously on bankruptcy. The last sets of variations in this edition were nearly complete by 1788, the same year he wrote his final three symphonies.

In the last year and a half of his life, Mozart's health steadily declined, but his productivity did not. Works from this time include the operas *Die Zauberflöte*, and *La clemenza di Tito*; his last piano concerto and the great clarinet concerto; and the partially complete Requiem. The story of the Requiem has been told in many forms, but the truth is somewhat short. The wealthy Count Walsegg-Stuppach commissioned through a messenger a Requiem Mass for his wife. The Count intended to claim the Requiem as his own composition. Mozart may or may not have held superstitions about this commission, though some say he feared that he had been poisoned. He lived long enough to see a rehearsal of portions of the work and left instructions for it's completion with his student and associate Franz Xaver Sussmayer.

Mozart died quietly on December 5, 1791, and was buried without fanfare.

It is difficult to imagine that Mozart's music could have gone in and out of "fashion" during his life, but the evidence clearly points in such a direction. It may even be that the memory of Mozart would be much less clear if it were not for the tireless efforts of Constanze Mozart. The musical world owes a great debt to her for her successful publication of his works, and arrangements of concerts in his memory.

—*Matthew Edwards*
editor

PERFORMANCE NOTES

Introduction to the Theme and Variation

The form now known as "Theme and Variations" has long been a favorite device of composers since the Baroque era. Some early versions, like the Passacaglia, presented a single bass line, over which melodic or other figuration was written. The upper voices/lines progressed through a series of variations as the bass remained constant. The Chaconne, another related form typically used a harmonic pattern as the consistent element below the freely changing material in the upper voices.

In Mozart's time a Theme and Variation set was usually based on an existing or original tune. Often, the first statement was the simplest, in order to clearly familiarize the listener with the theme and the underlying harmonies. From there, the variations began with countless options. Sometimes the melody was stated as clearly as the original, while the accompanimental patterns changed. In other cases the melody changed, or evolved, and only the harmony could be recognized. For many composers, these works provided an opportunity to show off not only their technical skill at the keyboard, but also their creative skill as a composer.

This collection contains only two sets of variations with tunes written by Mozart. The other six are themes borrowed from other composers. This was surely seen as a great compliment, to be the subject of variations by the great Mozart.

Performance Notes

An exhaustive guide to the performance practices of Mozart's works would surely fill more than one bookcase; a far shorter version must suffice here. While there may indeed be limitless items to consider when preparing these works, the following thoughts will at least touch on a few of the more significant points.

Mozart's Instruments

While one might assume that Mozart wrote all of his keyboard works for what we now know as the piano, this is not the case. The origins of the piano go back to 1700, an invention by the harpsichord-maker Bartolomeo Cristofori. His creation of a stringed keyboard instrument with dynamic shading was a significant, but not necessarily instant success. Over the years many piano-makers appeared, among them, the great names of Silbermann and Stein. Yet the harpsichord, with its long history and prolific number, remained the instrument of choice well into the middle of the eighteenth century. Bach himself was shown a Silbermann piano and is said not to have cared for the sound of the upper register. Therefore, it should come as little surprise that Mozart's early life was spent playing and writing for the harpsichord.

> There is no evidence that young Mozart, on tour or at home, at any time up to his final return from Italy in 1773, played in public any clavier but the harpsichord. It seems safe to say, therefore, that all the compositions for or with clavier written by him during this period were intended for the harpsichord.[1]

The complete lack of dynamic indication in the K.25 Variations seems to agree with this statement.

In the Fall of 1777 Mozart wrote a letter to his father in which he describes having played six of his sonatas on a piano made by Stein. He writes that "...the last one...sounds absolutely great on Stein's Piano forte.[2] Through his letters, and by his specification of certain works to be played on the "Piano-Forte," it can be gathered that by 1777 Mozart was writing exclusively for the piano.

Ornamentation

A great deal of research and opinions are available on late eighteenth century ornamentation. Yet, while it is important to be familiar with the current conventional wisdom, one cannot forget the fundamental principle that ornaments are decorative and improvisatory. They are decorative in the sense that they are subservient to the primary line, and improvisatory in that their execution varies—slightly or greatly—from performer to performer. In the Baroque era Johann Sebastian Bach wrote a very detailed chart explaining the ornamentation in his works. Yet Sandra Rosenblum, in her extremely helpful book *Performance Practices in Classic Piano Music* states that "Neither Haydn, Mozart, nor Beethoven left any systematic instructions for the performance of ornaments."[3] Clementi is perhaps the most significant composer to write instructions on ornamentation. Rosenblum further states that "Although many treatises discussed ornaments and gave instructions for their performance, there was not—and is not now—complete agreement regarding either notation or performance."[4] The point is that while there may be some general "rules" about the execution of turns, trills, and appoggiaturas, there are still many valid variables left to the unique and instinctive choice of each performer.

The following are a few general observations about some of the most common markings in these variations. Keep in mind that these are general suggestions, and that the context of each passage will be the final determining factor in the choice of execution.

THE SHORT AND LONG APPOGGIATURA

The short appoggiatura is usually seen as a small sixteenth note that may or may not have a slash through the stem. It typically occurs before a series of faster note values. It is often played quickly, sounding nearly attached to the next note. This is not a fixed rule, however, as some passages using this same notation are more appropriately executed as a long appoggiatura.

The typical long appoggiatura is more variable in length, receiving "one-half of a duple note or two-thirds of a note divisible by three."[5] Additionally, each of these could be longer or shorter, depending on the surrounding musical context, and suitability of expression. When seen as a small quarter note, as in the illustration below, it can share evenly the value of the half note, or be held for longer.

ILLUSTRATION: K.25, mm. 3–4

Another common occurrence is seen in the next illustration, traditionally executed as four sixteenth notes.

ILLUSTRATION: K.180, m. 98.

TRILLS

There are so many options available for trills; but the goal should always be an ornament that enhances the melody, and creates a smooth line. Here are three primary elements to consider:

- Trills can begin on the note indicated or on the note above. On this, Rosenblum says, "Until about 1800 the trill beginning with the upper auxiliary may still have been used more frequently, although possibly less for Mozart than for Haydn and Clementi."[6] While this may be most common, many factors exist which would allow for a trill to begin on the given note, including trills on dissonant notes, bass trills, and consecutive trills in an ascending or descending line.

- Most commonly, trills continue until the end of the note value, although Clementi illustrated the possibility of ending sooner if so desired.

- Often composers will indicate a specific conclusion to a trill by writing a closing turn or anticipation of the next note. Yet again, "If such a termination was not indicated, the performer was expected to add one where it would fit and be advantageous, particularly in effecting a smoother transition from the trill back to the melodic line."[7]

The question often arises about whether an ornament begins on the beat, or before. Rosenblum states, "...although the majority of ornaments in the Classic style were illustrated in tutors as beginning on the beat, those indicated with small notes were sometimes played before or after the beat."[8] This again reflects the flexibility available to the performer.

Other Topics

TEMPOS WITHIN THE VARIATIONS

Many variations within these works contain specific tempo indications, altering the speed from that which was presented in the first statement of the theme. Clearly, in these cases, the composer's wishes must be observed. For all of the others with no such indications, the tempo should generally be close to that of the theme. However, it cannot be ruled out that there are some changes of tempo within the variations. The best tempo for a given variation may indeed be somewhat different from the original in order to best capture its unique character.

PEDAL

Care should be taken not to be too free with the pedal in these works. Pedaling heavily through scales and other passage-work will result in a very blurry sound, compromising the clarity of Mozart's writing.

REPEAT SIGNS

In works with repeat signs, the most common practice is to repeat only the opening section. The choice may also be made to repeat both sections, or not to repeat at all. If the opening passage is short, such as a single phrase, it may require the repeat; alternatively, if the melody is longer, and contains more than one phrase, a repeat may not be necessary.

FINGERINGS

All fingerings are added by the editor.

Notes on the Variations

Seven Variations on "Willem van Nassau," K. 25

COMPOSED IN 1766

These variations hardly sound as if they were written by a ten-year old boy. The innate charm of Mozart is present, but there are some clear differences of style when compared to the other works in this collection. The title indicates that the theme is from the Dutch national anthem of the period. (The anthem sung today is fairly different from the subject of this piece.) As discussed above, this work was almost surely written for the harpsichord. With this in mind, the pedal could be left out entirely, or used only sparingly for the most necessary moments. There is a good

deal of ornamentation in this work which should be carefully thought out. One slightly unusual marking for this era is the mordent designation in the first measure. While generally performed as a descending single or double shake as in the Baroque, it is equally possible to perform it as a short trill or even a turn. In general, the melody is clearly present and prominent in each variation; the third variation is the exception, focusing more on the harmony than the melodic subject.

Six Variations on "Mio caro Adone," K. 180

COMPOSED IN 1773

Translated as "My dear Adonis," this theme is taken from the opera *La fiera di Venezia* by Antonio Salieri (1750–1825). This opera was one of Salieri's most successful, and melodies from it would have been well-known at the time. Written seven years after the "Nassau" variations, this work clearly illustrates Mozart's growth as a composer. We begin to hear the lyrical and elegant writing that characterizes his mature style.

One of the most interesting elements of this work is the transformation of the theme. The opening statement, a beautiful vocal line, is molded and shaped throughout each variation. This transformation does not necessarily progress from "most similar to the original" to "least similar." Mozart instead crafts a new view of the theme with each variation, creating a small set of unique character pieces. The primary stability comes from the theme.

There are a great number of dynamic markings (specifically *forte* and *piano*) in this work, more than are typically seen in Mozart's keyboard works. Clearly, the performer will want to play with more than two levels of volume, so the markings should be considered in the context of each variation. Additionally, be careful not to change with such suddenness as to break the focus of the melodic line.

There are increased technical difficulties here as compared to the "Nassau" variations, particularly in variations four and six. For variation four, keep the hand relaxed to better negotiate the leap between the trills. Variation six may only pose a difficulty if a quick tempo is chosen, especially in the left hand of measures 105–107. The solution here is a good, even rotation of the wrist and forearm, as one does for tremolo octaves. Practice the outer notes only before including the interval.

Twelve Variations on a Menuett, K. 179
COMPOSED IN 1774

Johann Fischer (1733–1800) was an accomplished German oboist, who wrote several concertos and other chamber works. This theme comes from the last movement of one of his oboe concertos. Mozart played these variations frequently throughout his life; indeed, the wide range of technical demands make this a dramatic and exciting set.[9]

One can almost hear the oboe playing the melody, and the articulations and ornaments seem to have been carefully placed with this instrument in mind. The first of the more difficult variations is number 4, in which the tremolo figure exists in nearly every measure. Steady rotation is key, and when the interval is only a second, some may find it suits the hand better to use a 4-3 fingering, rather than 5-4, as in measure 109. Remember to keep the focus on the note that is moving, and not the one that is repeated.

Variation nine poses difficulty, with the two-octave leaps as in measure 227. It is important to avoid a harsh and sudden accent on either the last upper note, or the first lower note. This often happens as one feels the need to hurry to the next location by "pushing off" the upper, or "crash-landing" on the lower. Stay focused on the upper note until it is complete, then move quickly with careful preparation for the volume of the lower note. Adjust the tempo as needed to navigate this difficult variation.

When practicing variation ten one may first see only the octaves in the tremolo passages. While it would be effective to practice these passages by "blocking" (playing together) the octaves, it is also very important to practice the other distances in the sections, that occur when the octaves are moving. An example of this is in measure 264: the distance between the second and third sixteenth notes. These sevenths and ninths are just different enough in size from the octaves that they can be easily missed without careful attention.

The Adagio of variation eleven is almost operatic in its lyricism. The difficulty lies in staying focused on the melody in a very slow-moving harmonic progression. One must mentally sing the line in order to give it the proper shape.

Twelve Variations on "Ah, vous dirai-je Maman," K. 265
COMPOSED IN 1781–82

Known best to Americans as "Twinkle, Twinkle, Little Star," this tune was quite popular in Mozart's day. Below are the French lyrics, with translation:

> *Ah! Vous dirai-je Maman*
> Ah! Will I tell you, Mommy
>
> *Ce qui cause mon tourment ?*
> What is tormenting me?
>
> *Papa veut que je raisonne*
> Daddy wants me to reason
>
> *Comme une grande personne.*
> Like a grown up person.
>
> *Moi je dis que les bonbons*
> Me, I say that sweets
>
> *Valent mieux que la raison.*
> Are worth more than reason.

The opening statement of the theme is perfectly simple, completely suitable for these lyrics. What follows is nearly a catalogue of pedagogical technique, providing exercises for rapid passage-work, tremolos, articulations, and precise voicing. The final variation is a grand flourish to round out the set.

In variations two, four, and eight, observe carefully the tied notes, holding them without tension in the hand, which will allow you to gently resolve the moving notes.

In variation six, at measure 154, voice the top of the left hand chords, where the melody has shifted, while the right hand is ornamenting with sixteenth notes.

Variation twelve provides an excellent etude on finger-crossing, particularly second over thumb. Play these gently, without forcing them. Also be careful not to harshly accent the third beat of measures such as 302 and 303. The sudden leap outward often causes a shift in volume, if not approached with a relaxed hand.

Twelve Variations on "La belle Françoise," K. 353
COMPOSED IN 1781–82

The source of this theme is somewhat more obscure. According to Sir William Glock, the melody comes from an illustration in a book commemorating the death of the Duke of Marlboro.[10] The image is of an English soldier bidding farewell to his love. Underneath are the words "Adieu donc, Dame françoise" (Goodbye, then, my French lady) set to the melody given here.[11]

The melody is freely treated throughout, and Mozart carefully crafts each variation with its own unique character. Triplet rhythms abound, in deference to the compound meter of the subject, yet great variety is achieved in the presentation of those rhythms. Metrical change comes only in the last variation, in a brief switch to two-four time. The set closes with a simple return to the original theme, with a short codetta to confirm the end.

In variation one, be careful not to accent the thirty-second notes; play each one gently, nearly equal with the following dotted sixteenth. Shape the line by mentally singing through the rests.

In variation two, the shape of the left hand should generally follow that of the right; don't break that shape with unnecessary accents at either the beginning or end of the sixteenth note patterns.

Variation eight should not sound like a technical exercise. Keep the melody in the eighth notes lyrical, and the left hand octaves firm and supportive.

Eight Variations on a March from *Les mariages samnites*, K. 352

COMPOSED IN 1781

The title of this theme is "Dieu d'amour" (God of Love) by Andre-Ernest-Modeste Gretry (1741–1813), and contained in his opera *The Samnite Marriages*. Gretry was a successful and well-respected composer, with a strong influence on comic opera of his time.

Play the opening chords strongly, but not harshly. The theme is definitely a March, but with a solemn and somewhat gentle character. One of the most beautiful elements of this theme is the inclusion of the half-step B-natural, as seen in the first measure of variation one. This "sigh-motive" reappears in variations three, five, seven, and eight, contributing to a certain tenderness of the theme.

Six Variations on an Allegretto, K. 54

COMPOSED IN 1788

This work is the first of only two in this collection utilizing an original theme. These variations also exist as the last movement of the Sonata in F Major for Piano and Violin, K. 547, written in the same month as the keyboard version.[12] The keyboard parts of both works are nearly identical, with the most significant change appearing in the

fourth variation. In the Sonata, the violin does little more than assist the piano, but does finally get the melody in the fourth variation. As a result, Mozart rescores this in the keyboard work in order to keep the melody present.

Six Variations on a Theme from the Clarinet Quintet K. 581, K. Anh. 137

COMPOSED IN 1789

This work is also on an original theme, and is taken directly from one of Mozart's existing works. The Clarinet Quintet is scored for clarinet and strings, and the last movement is the basis for these variations. The work here is probably best described as an arrangement, as the instrumental parts have been condensed to fit the hands, and some other alterations have also been made, presumably to make the work more pianistic. Mozart may have created this piano arrangement, but there is no evidence to confirm the authorship.

Closing Thoughts

It has been said that "Mozart is too easy for children, and too hard for adults." At first, this is a shocking phrase, but as one considers it, there is truth on many levels. In the best sense, it conveys a subtle reminder about the purity and simplicity of his work. Mozart's music is full of life and spirit, rapturous and effusive, and always entertaining. Yet it is often easy to become so mesmerized with the musical and technical perfection of his writing skill, that we lose sight of the true and simple beauty of the works. Clearly, accurate technique is critical to a good performance, yet when that element consumes the performer's concentration, most of the aesthetic value of the work is lost. As a wise teacher once said: "Never forget the joyous sound of the music!"

As I often write about my recordings, please remember that what you hear on the recording is a spontaneous moment in time. While it is true that a great deal of study has gone into the preparation of this recording, one cannot ever forbid the possibility of sudden inspiration. When we perform the works of these great composers, I like to think of the analogy that we are conversing with the composer, and musically discussing their work. This recording then, is my own conversation with Mozart.

—Matthew Edwards
editor

Notes

1 Broder, Nathan. "Mozart and the 'Clavier.'" *The Musical Quarterly*, Vol. 27, No. 4 (October 1941): 422-32.

2 Spaethling, Robert. *Mozart's Letters, Mozart's Life: Selected Letters*. trans. Robert Spaethling (New York: W. W. Norton, 2000), 78.

3 Rosenblum, Sandra. *Performance Practices in Classic Piano Music* (Bloomington: Indiana University Press, 1988), 216.

4 Ibid., 217.

5 Ibid., 224.

6 Ibid., 245.

7 Ibid., 241.

8 Ibid., 218.

9 Zaslaw, Neal, with William Cowdery, eds. *The Compleat Mozart: A Guide to the Musical Works of Wolfgang Amadeus Mozart* (New York: W.W. Norton, 1990), 318.

10 This may have been the third Duke of Marlboro, Charles Spencer, born in 1706 and died in 1758.

11 Zaslaw, Neal, with William Cowdery, eds. *The Compleat Mozart: A Guide to the Musical Works of Wolfgang Amadeus Mozart* (New York: W.W. Norton, 1990), 319.

12 Ibid., 320.

For Further Reading

Brown, Clive. *Classical and Romantic Performing Practice, 1750–1900*. Oxford: Oxford University Press, 2004.

Lawson, Colin, and Robin Stowell. *The Historical Performance of Music: An Introduction*. Cambridge: Cambridge University Press, 1999.

Neumann, Frederick. *Ornamentation in Baroque and Post-Baroque Music: With Special Emphasis on J. S. Bach*. Princeton: Princeton University Press, 1978.

Rosen, Charles. The Classical Style. New York: W. W. Norton, 1998.

Rosenblum, Sandra. *Performance Practices in Classic Piano Music*. Bloomington: Indiana University Press, 1988.

Solomon, Manyard. *Mozart: A Life*. New York: Harper Collins, 1995.

Spaethling, Robert. *Mozart's Letters, Mozart's Life: Selected Letters*. trans. Robert Spaethling. New York: W. W. Norton, 2000.

Zaslaw, Neal, with William Cowdery, eds. *The Compleat Mozart: A Guide to the Musical Works of Wolfgang Amadeus Mozart*. New York: W.W. Norton, 1990.

Seven Variations
on "Willem van Nassau"

Wolfgang Amadeus Mozart
K. 25

AIR

VAR. I

VAR. II

VAR. III

VAR. VI

Six Variations
on "Mio caro Adone"

Wolfgang Amadeus Mozart
K. 180

MENUETTO

Andante

VAR. II

VAR. III

VAR. IV

VAR. VI

Allegretto

Twelve Variations
on a Menuett

Wolfgang Amadeus Mozart
K. 179

VAR. I

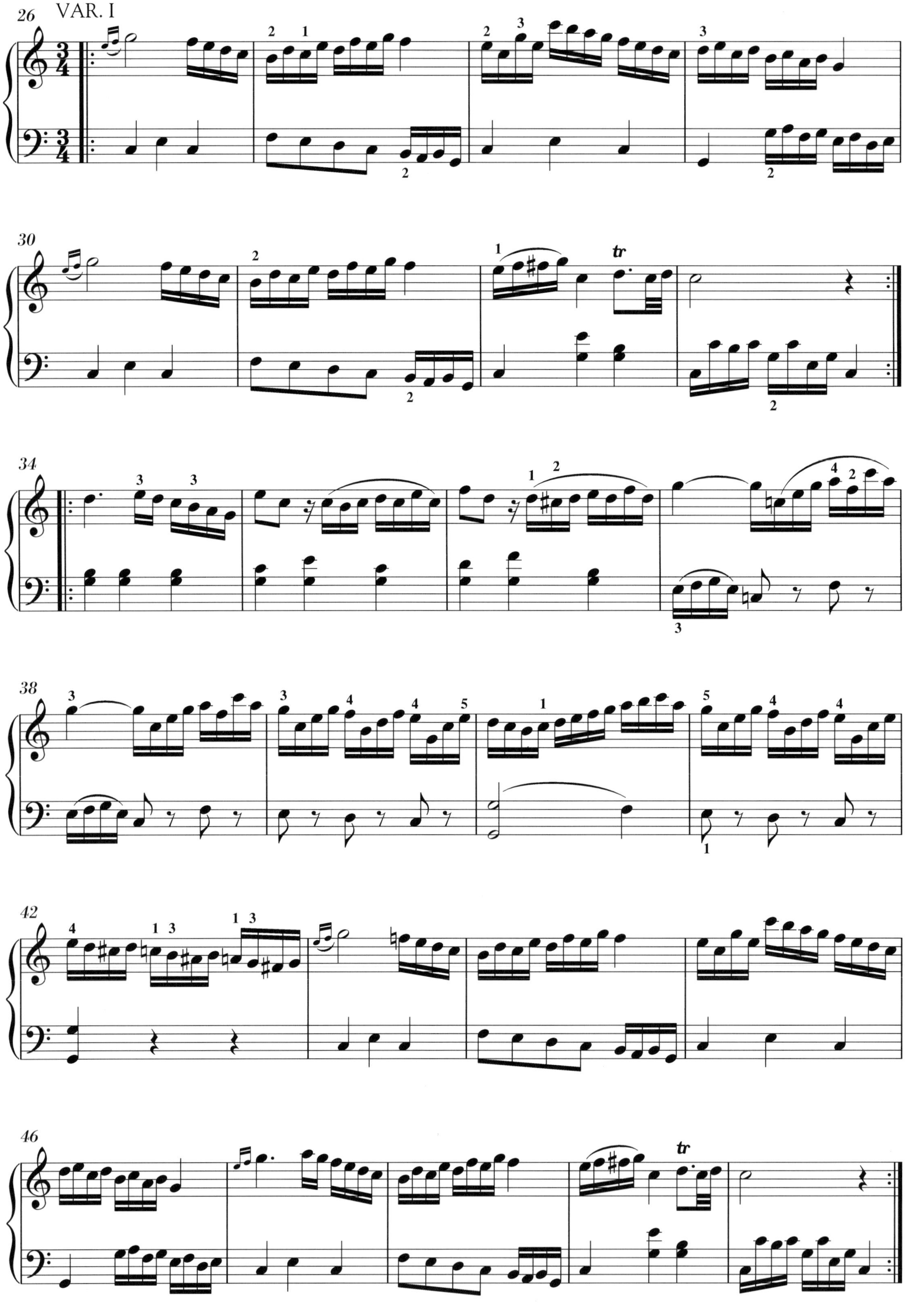

VAR. II

VAR. III

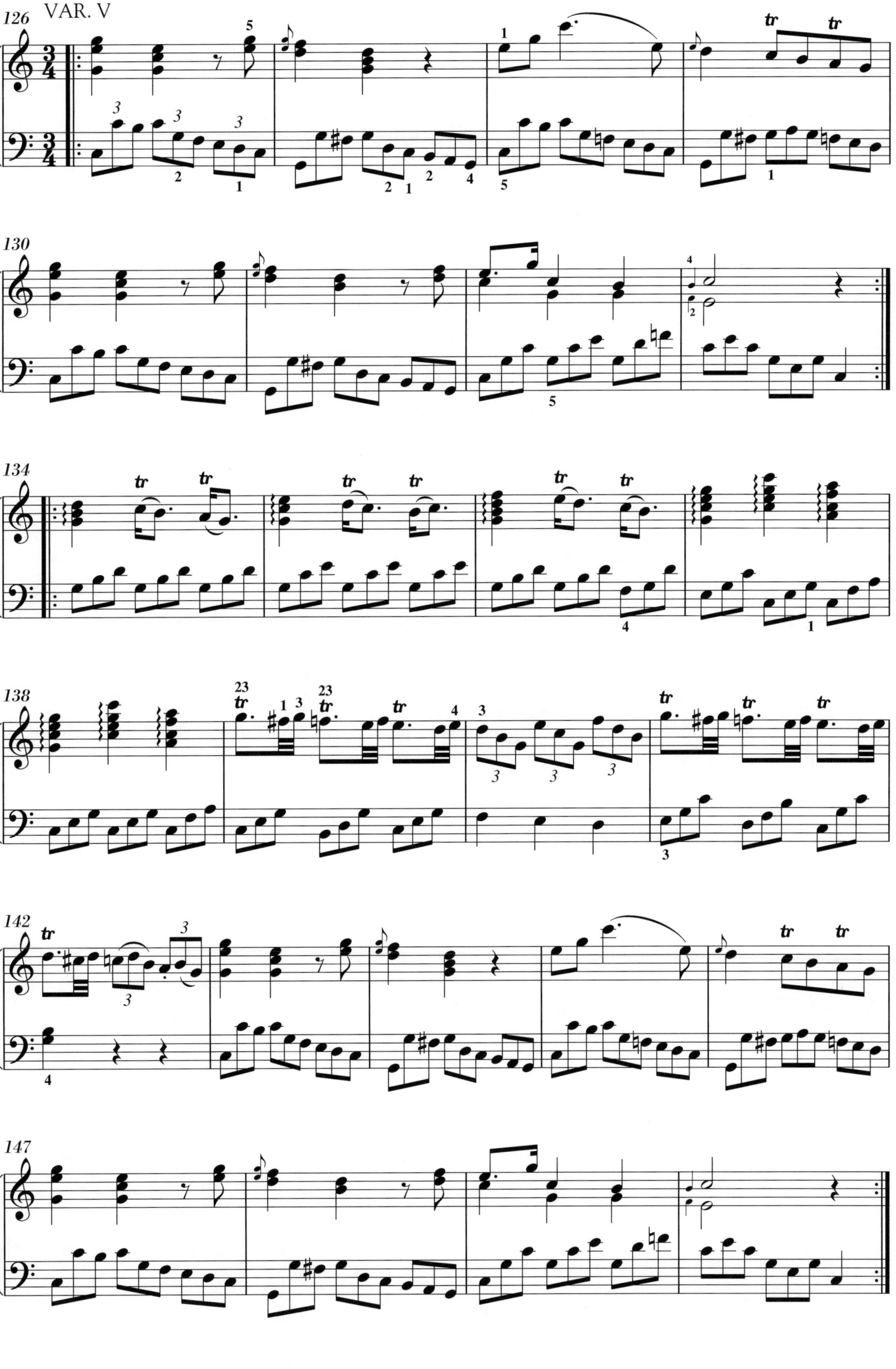
VAR. V

VAR. VII

VAR. VIII

VAR. IX

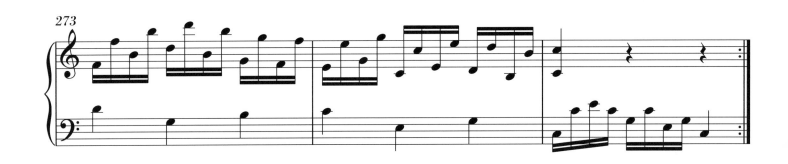

VAR. XI

VAR. XII

Twelve Variations
on "Ah, vous dirai-je Maman"
("Twinkle, Twinkle, Little Star")

Wolfgang Amadeus Mozart
K. 265

THEMA
[Andante]

VAR. I

VAR. II

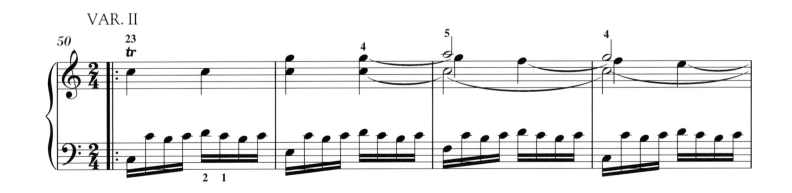

VAR. III

VAR. V

VAR. VII

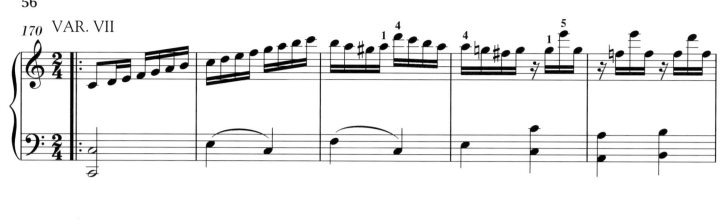

218 VAR. IX

224

230

236

242 VAR. X

VAR. XI

VAR. XII

Twelve Variations
on "La belle Françoise"

Wolfgang Amadeus Mozart
K. 353

THEMA

[Adagio]

VAR. I

VAR. III

VAR. VI

VAR. VIII

VAR. XI

Adagio

VAR. XII

Presto

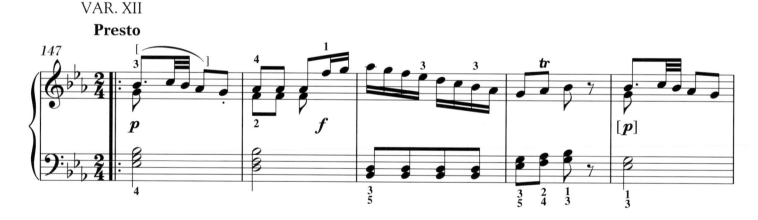

Eight Variations
on a March from *Les mariages samnites*

Wolfgang Amadeus Mozart
K. 352

VAR. IV

VAR. VII

VAR. VIII

Six Variations
on an Allegretto

Wolfgang Amadeus Mozart
K. 54

THEMA
[Moderato]

VAR. I

Six Variations
on a Theme from the Clarinet Quintet, K. 581

Wolfgang Amadeus Mozart
K. Anh. 137

VAR. I

VAR. II

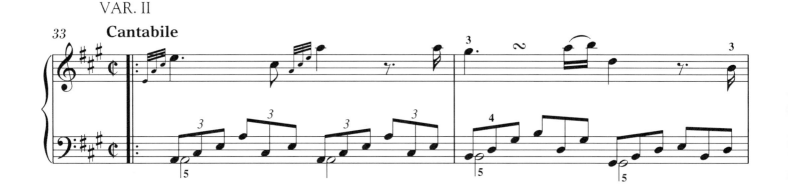

VAR. III

VAR. VI

Maggiore

VAR. V

Adagio

100

attacca subito

VAR. VI

Allegro

ABOUT THE EDITOR
MATTHEW EDWARDS

Dr. T. Matthew Edwards is a musician of many facets. As a pianist, he has been hailed by critics for his "...considerable talent...honest musicianship, and a formidable technique." His performances have taken him throughout the United States and to Asia, appearing as recitalist, guest artist, concerto soloist, and collaborative artist. His competition winnings include the Grand Prize in the Stravinsky Awards International Competition, and First Prize in the Music Teachers National Association National Collegiate Finals. He has previously served as part-time faculty at several colleges, including the Peabody Conservatory of Music in Baltimore, and full-time as Assistant Professor of Music at Anne Arundel Community College (AACC) in Maryland. Currently, he is Associate Professor of Music and Director of Keyboard Studies at Missouri Western State University. As a lecturer, he has been featured at the National Conference of the Music Teachers National Association, the World Piano Pedagogy Conference, and at the state conventions of the Maryland, Missouri, and Texas Music Teacher's Association. He also serves on the editorial committee for American Music Teacher magazine. As a composer, he has had major works premiered in Chicago, Salt Lake City, and the Baltimore area, and is a contributing author for the Hal Leonard Student Piano Library. As a conductor and coach, Dr. Edwards has served as the rehearsal pianist/coach for the Annapolis Opera, and musical director for Opera AACC. He lives in Kansas City, Missouri with his wife, Kelly, and their three children, Audrey, Jackson, and Cole.